TWIN TOWERS REMEMBERED

LOWER MANHATTAN SKYLINE FROM THE BROOKLYN SIDE OF THE WILLIAMSBURG BRIDGE, AUGUST 21, 2001

TWIN TOWERS REMEMBERED

CAMILO JOSÉ VERGARA

PRINCETON ARCHITECTURAL PRESS   NATIONAL BUILDING MUSEUM

NEW YORK   WASHINGTON, D.C.

PUBLISHED BY

Princeton Architectural Press

37 East Seventh Street

New York, New York 10003

For a free catalog of books, call 1.800.722.6657.

Visit our web site at www.papress.com.

PROJECT EDITOR: Clare Jacobson

PRODUCTION EDITOR AND DESIGNER: Sara E. Stemen

SPECIAL THANKS TO: Nettie Aljian, Ann Alter, Amanda Atkins, Nicola Bednarek, Janet Behning, Penny Chu, Jan Cigliano, Jane Garvie, Tom Hutten, Mark Lamster, Nancy Eklund Later, Linda Lee, Brook Schneider, Evan Schoninger, Lottchen Shivers, Jennifer Thompson, and Deb Wood of Princeton Architectural Press   —Kevin C. Lippert, publisher

ISBN 1-56898-351-4

LOWER MANHATTAN SKYLINE FROM EXCHANGE PLACE,

JERSEY CITY, NEW JERSEY, 1977

WORLD TRADE CENTER FROM TRIBECA, MANHATTAN, 1983

Although the Princeton Architectural Press offices are downtown in New York's East Village, we couldn't see the World Trade Center towers from our windows. But we all saw them on our way to work, and, like millions of other New Yorkers on September 11, stood in disbelief at the corner, or huddled around the radio in our office, or just went home, because no one felt like working, and what we were doing suddenly felt completely irrelevant.

Since then, the question all New Yorkers, indeed people all around the world, keep asking—"What can we do to help?"—seems partly an effort to recover relevance in the face of something so unspeakable that it shakes your fundamental beliefs about humanity and your place in it.

It first occurred to us to put together a small, dispassionate book documenting the World Trade Center, just to preserve information about the buildings. At about the same time, I received a phone call from Camilo José Vergara, author of our book *Silent Cities*. Camilo arrived in New York City just as the Twin Towers were under construction, and has photographed them for the last thirty-one years. Most of his shots, taken from New York's outer boroughs or New Jersey, show the towers rising from the New York skyline. Sometimes they serve as the background for busy streetscapes or abandoned car lots, or for pictures of his children playing, but all of his photographs remind us of how vibrant and strong a presence these buildings were, no matter where you stood. This was no detached documentation, but a moving and personal memorial to the now-fallen towers.

There was much discussion in our office about whether to publish such a book at this time. But making books about architecture is what we do, and ultimately this seemed to be the most direct way for us to offer assistance. We are donating all profits from the sale of this book to the American Red Cross. We hope this contribution, however modest, helps those who need it. We hope, too, that this tribute helps us all remember the buildings that, defying belief, are now gone.

Kevin C. Lippert
Princeton Architectural Press
October 2001

LOWER MANHATTAN SKYLINE FROM EXCHANGE PLACE, 1977

All of us at the National Building Museum are proud to exhibit Camilo José Vergara's poignant photographs of the World Trade Center.

For over thirty years, Camilo photographed the Twin Towers, designed by the architects Minoru Yamasaki and Emery Roth & Sons and engineered by Leslie Robertson of Skilling, Helle, Christiansen, Robertson. Camilo's photographs reveal the architects' and engineers' work in all its complexity, and become the perfect means for communicating an enduring aspect of the museum's mission: the celebration of American buildings and builders. These images allow us to fully grasp the Twin Towers' physical size, their symbolic magnitude, and, ultimately, the daunting immensity of our collective loss. In this sense, this book and the exhibition have a restorative dimension. And maybe that reveals another, less obvious reason for embarking on these projects in the first place: We believe that by helping to disseminate Camilo's photographs, we are participating in a process of healing.

I would like to thank all those individuals who helped to realize these undertakings. I am particularly indebted to Howard Decker, Chief Curator at the museum, and Thomas Mellins, Guest Curator for the exhibition.

Susan Henshaw Jones
National Building Museum
October 2001

MEMORIAL, UNION SQUARE, MANHATTAN, SEPTEMBER 2001

"The essence of New York is tall buildings."

—KENNETH T. JACKSON

I have been photographing the World Trade Center towers since 1970, when they were first under construction. My intention was to record them from every possible angle, during different times of day, and in different seasons. I did this just because I liked them.

The two tall slabs seemed to me like stakes holding Manhattan in place. Did the island rise a little at its southern end when the World Trade Center buildings disintegrated amidst immense clouds of dust? How would I find my bearings now in Newark or Brownsville, without the silvery towers as reference points? The demolition itself puzzled me: were the towers made of sham steel? How could something so enormous be brought down so quickly? Their shapes appeared as simple as the old headstones in New England cemeteries, and they became even simpler as one moved away and lost sight of the details. From the start, their form suggested a memorial, but what they memorialized was a mystery. The last thing I ever imagined was that I would outlive these buildings.

Individuality—the clamoring ego of a single thrusting identity—is the arrogance of skyscrapers. But these were twins: Tower One and Tower Two; another set of smaller buildings raised the number to seven, making an architectural family. I warmed to the buildings when my children were born, and I photographed their baby flesh against the structures' hardness. As my children grew up, I wanted the towers to give them a sense of sublimity; for the same reason, I took them to California's Redwood Forest. I was saying to them: "See something big. Perhaps a god exists who is even bigger, and perhaps as indifferent."

To many the towers symbolized the aspirations of this capital of capitalism. At first, the contrast between their sleek, costly expanses rising in the midst of vacant lots and warehouses where the homeless congregated struck me as another sign of New York's insensitivity to the poor. But later, I grew to see the towers as great creations. Sometimes on cold days, their silver color made them look like hard, menacing blades. At other times they reflected the clouds. They became upright fields of amber on late afternoons in winter. Yet like many other people, I hesitated to call them beautiful. For hard-core aesthetes the World Trade Center towers were worthwhile only as a vantage point from which to look out. Some limited their praise to the space in between the structures. Most see no point in criticizing them now and turn respectful attention to the dead.

I best liked seeing the towers from Exchange Place in Jersey City. Before the World Financial Center was built, they soared from the water. The Hudson River seemed to overlap their base as they rose behind chimneys, masts, and radar installations. People on the decks of passing boats invariably had their backs to me as they looked at the towers. Sitting on a rotten pier in New Jersey, I contemplated how the minimalism of the World Trade Center blended with the classical temples, pyramidal roofs, church domes, and dancing statues perched atop neighboring early twentieth-century skyscrapers. The lower Manhattan skyline with its extraordinary juxtapositions of past forms and present-day rationalist architecture—the latter gaining from the former—was one of the most inspiring architectural assemblages I had ever seen.

People called the towers majestic. But since the early nineties it had been possible to see them whole only from the World Trade Center Plaza. Even then, looking straight up at the buildings distorted their forms and was uncomfortable. Except for the addition of an antenna, the structures remained unchanged. Yet they had long stopped being isolated citadels; they had become a friendly landmark. The population that used them changed as families moved to the area; by the time they were destroyed, they were the focal point of a lively community of residents and commuters in a neighborhood of restaurants, cultural activities, and recreational spaces.

The towers lost some of their presence when they began to harmonize with their newer neighbors. No more could they double their size on calm days by being reflected in the Hudson River. Yet still they had the capacity to surprise by appearing in strange places: above a junkyard in Jersey City, at the end of a street in Williamsburg, Brooklyn, or above a nature preserve in Jamaica Bay, Queens. They had grandeur when seen from the Brooklyn side of the Manhattan Bridge and offered surprise as slivers, streamlined and

4   CHARLES AND VIRGINIA SEEN AGAINST THE TOWERS OF THE WORLD TRADE CENTER, 1986

simple, compared to the smaller buildings around Battery Park.

After the towers collapsed, passengers riding the subways across the Manhattan Bridge would stand up when the skyline appeared to look at the gap they left. From New Jersey, five buildings now dominate the lower Manhattan skyline: the four bulky towers of the World Financial Center framing the long-hidden, neo-Gothic Woolworth Building, an unquestionable architectural beauty. In contrast, the large dome atop one of the Financial Center towers reminds me of the visionary funereal designs of the eighteenth-century French architect Etienne-Louis Boullée, the tranquility of its curve for a week marred by smoke.

I was unaware of the intensity of my interest in the towers until they disappeared. My personal response to this tragedy has been to put together a chronicle of the buildings; in an effort to hold on to them, I have searched for every photograph I ever took of the towers, and at the same time I have documented the effect of their absence on the skyline. *Twin Towers Remembered* gives glimpses of these amazing buildings, of the extraordinary region they dominated, and of the void they left behind.

Camilo José Vergara
October 2001

PHOTOGRAPHIC SITES

NUMBERS REFER TO PAGES ON WHICH IMAGES APPEAR.

★ World Trade Center site 4, 8, 14 LEFT AND RIGHT, 15 LEFT AND RIGHT, 60, 61, 62, 63, 74, 75

A George Washington Bridge 86

B South Bronx 24 LEFT

C Hell Gate 50

D Kearny, New Jersey 31

E Pulaski Skyway 32

F Hoboken, New Jersey 22

G Grove Street area, Jersey City, New Jersey 10, 18, 28, 30, 72

H South Jersey City 33

I South shoreline, Jersey City GATEFOLD PANEL A, 10, 11, 39, 41, 68 LEFT AND RIGHT, 69 LEFT

J Exchange Placc, Jersey City v, viii, 7, 13, 35, 44 LEFT AND RIGHT, 46, 64, 65, 69 RIGHT, 71, 79

K New Jersey ferries 49, 56

L Staten Island Ferry GATEFOLD PANEL B, GATEFOLD PANEL D

M Liberty Island 48, 66

N Statue of Liberty Ferry GATE-FOLD PANEL C, 58

O Union Square, Manhattan x, 81

P Tribeca, Manhattan vi, 3

Q Center Street, Manhattan 78

R Wall Street/South Street Seaport area, Manhattan 56, 58, 80

S Red Hook, Brooklyn 42, 43

T Brooklyn Heights, Brooklyn 26, 54

U Brooklyn Bridge 52, 53

V Manhattan Bridge 12, 76, 77, 82–85

W DUMBO, Brooklyn 16, 17, 38

X Williamsburg, Brooklyn 27

Y Bedford-Stuyvesant, Brooklyn 20, 21

Z Brownsville, Brooklyn 23. 24 RIGHT

* Broad Channel, Jamaica Bay, Queens 36

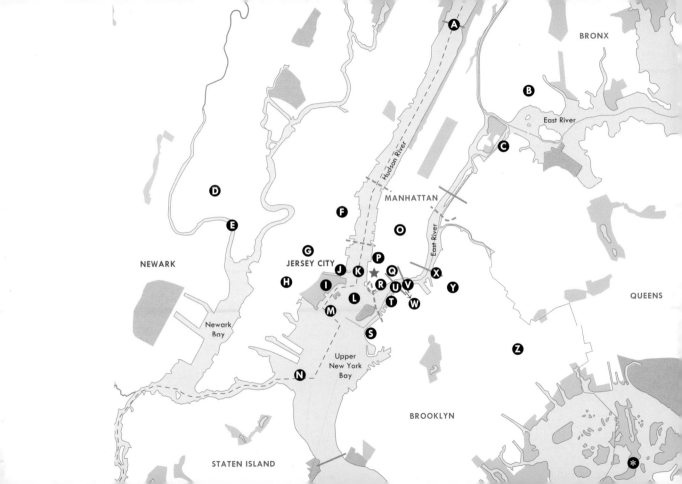

LOWER MANHATTAN
SKYLINE FROM THE
WATERFRONT, SOUTH
JERSEY CITY, 1977

LOWER MANHATTAN
SKYLINE FROM THE STATEN
ISLAND FERRY, 1989

CHARLES LOOKING AT
THE LOWER MANHATTAN
SKYLINE FROM THE STATUE
OF LIBERTY FERRY, 1985

LOWER MANHATTAN SKY-
LINE FROM THE STATEN
ISLAND FERRY, 2001

CONSTRUCTION

WORLD TRADE CENTER UNDER CONSTRUCTION, SEEN FROM WEST STREET, MANHATTAN, 1970

10 ABOVE AND OPPOSITE: LOWER MANHATTAN SKYLINE FROM SOUTH JERSEY CITY WATERFRONT, 1970

ABOVE: VIEW FROM SOUTH JERSEY CITY, 1970. OPPOSITE: VIEW FROM THE MANHATTAN BRIDGE, 1970

14 WORLD TRADE CENTER UNDER CONSTRUCTION, VIEW NORTH, MANHATTAN, 1970 (LEFT) AND IN 1985 (RIGHT)

ST. PAUL'S CHAPEL WITH THE WORLD TRADE CENTER UNDER CONSTRUCTION, 1970 (LEFT) AND AFTER ITS DESTRUCTION IN 2001 (RIGHT)   15

THE WORLD TRADE CENTER UNDER CONSTRUCTION FROM BETWEEN THE BROOKLYN AND MANHATTAN BRIDGES, BROOKLYN, 1970

VIEW FROM THE SAME LOCATION AFTER THE DESTRUCTION OF THE WORLD TRADE CENTER, OCTOBER 2001

NEIGHBORHOODS

LOWER MANHATTAN SKYLINE FROM SOUTH JERSEY CITY, 1977

20   LOWER MANHATTAN SKYLINE FROM THE TOMPKINS HOUSES IN BEDFORD-STUYVESANT, BROOKLYN, 1989

THE SAME VIEW FROM BEDFORD-STUYVESANT IN 2000

22   VIEW FROM HOBOKEN, NEW JERSEY, 1977 (ABOVE) AND FROM THE KINGSBORO HOUSES IN BROWNSVILLE, BROOKLYN, 1989 (OPPOSITE)

VIEW OF THE MANHATTAN SKYLINE FROM THE SOUTH BRONX, 1988 (LEFT) AND WEST FROM

THE ROOF OF THE LANGSTON HUGHES APARTMENTS IN BROWNSVILLE, BROOKLYN, 2001 (RIGHT)

LOWER MANHATTAN SKYLINE FROM BROOKLYN HEIGHTS, 1980

WORLD TRADE CENTER FROM THE ELEVATED MARCY AVENUE

SUBWAY STOP IN WILLIAMSBURG, BROOKLYN, 1977

28 WORLD TRADE CENTER FROM THE GROVE STREET AREA, JERSEY CITY, 1978

LOWER MANHATTAN FROM FOURTH STREET, EAST OF AVENUE B, EAST VILLAGE, MANHATTAN, 1990

ABOVE: VIEW FROM THE GROVE STREET AREA, JERSEY CITY, 1978. OPPOSITE: MANHATTAN SKYLINE FROM KEARNY, NEW JERSEY, 1980

32   LOWER MANHATTAN SKYLINE FROM THE PULASKI SKYWAY, NEW JERSEY MEADOWLANDS, 1980

LOWER MANHATTAN SKYLINE FROM SOUTH JERSEY CITY, 1977

WORLD TRADE CENTER FROM EXCHANGE PLACE, 1977

WATERWAYS, BRIDGES, AND BOATS

WORLD TRADE CENTER FROM JAMAICA BAY WILDLIFE REFUGE, BROAD CHANNEL, QUEENS, 1981

LOWER MANHATTAN SKYLINE FROM A SPOT JUST NORTH OF THE BROOKLYN BRIDGE, BROOKLYN, 1978

WORLD TRADE CENTER FROM THE SOUTH JERSEY CITY WATERFRONT, 1977

WORLD TRADE CENTER FROM FERRY BOAT GRAVEYARD ON THE SOUTH JERSEY CITY WATERFRONT, 1977

ABOVE AND OPPOSITE: THE FREIGHTER *COSTA RICA* AS IT APPROACHED LOWER MANHATTAN, SEEN FROM RED HOOK, BROOKLYN, 1978   43

OPPOSITE, LEFT: INDIAN FREIGHTER PASSING BY THE WORLD TRADE CENTER, SEEN FROM EXCHANGE PLACE, 1977

OPPOSITE, RIGHT: FOURTH OF JULY CELEBRATION, SEEN FROM EXCHANGE PLACE, 1978

VIEW FROM EXCHANGE PLACE AFTER THE DESTRUCTION

OF THE WORLD TRADE CENTER, SEPTEMBER 2001

LOWER MANHATTAN SKYLINE FROM THE STATUE OF LIBERTY FERRY, 1992 (OPPOSITE) AND OCTOBER 2001 (ABOVE)

WORLD TRADE CENTER FROM HELL GATE, EAST RIVER, 1989

52   LOWER MANHATTAN SKYLINE FROM THE BROOKLYN BRIDGE, 1977 (ABOVE) AND OCTOBER 2001 (OPPOSITE)

IN DETAIL

WORLD TRADE CENTER FROM BROOKLYN HEIGHTS, 1977

SECTION OF WORLD TRADE CENTER TOWER AND THE
STATUE KNOWN AS "GOLDEN BOY," WALL STREET AREA,
MANHATTAN, 1977

SECTION OF WORLD FINANCIAL CENTER TOWER

FLANKED BY THE WORLD TRADE CENTER TOWERS,

SEEN FROM THE HUDSON RIVER, 1991

ABOVE: LOWER MANHATTAN FROM WALL STREET AREA, 1977. OPPOSITE: LOWER MANHATTAN FROM STATUE OF LIBERTY FERRY, 1983

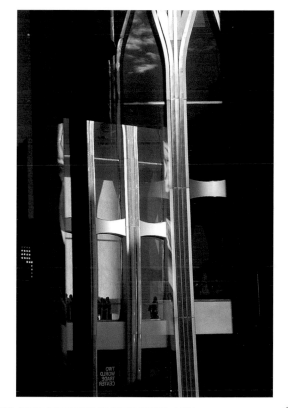

ABOVE: VIEWS FROM INSIDE ONE OF THE TWIN TOWERS, 1977. OPPOSITE: DETAIL OF THE WORLD TRADE CENTER, 1976

61

REFLECTION OF A WORLD TRADE CENTER TOWER

ON A WINDOW OF ST. PAUL'S CHAPEL, 1977

CHARLES AND VIRGINIA ON THE WORLD TRADE CENTER PLAZA (AUSTIN J. TOBIN PLAZA), 1985

64 DETAIL OF LOWER MANHATTAN FROM EXCHANGE PLACE, 1977

LOWER MANHATTAN SKYLINE FROM EXCHANGE PLACE, 1977

NATURE

LOWER MANHATTAN SKYLINE FROM LIBERTY ISLAND, 1986

68   LEFT AND RIGHT: LOWER MANHATTAN SKYLINE FROM SOUTH JERSEY CITY, 1977

LOWER MANHATTAN SKYLINE FROM SOUTH JERSEY CITY, 1979 (LEFT) AND FROM EXCHANGE PLACE, 1977 (RIGHT)

LOWER MANHATTAN SKYLINE FROM EXCHANGE PLACE, 1977

IN MEMORY

WORLD TRADE CENTER FROM THE GROVE STREET AREA, JERSEY CITY, 1977; A MEMORIAL
TO DECEASED MEMBERS OF THE JERSEY CITY POLICE DEPARTMENT IS IN THE FOREGROUND.

RIGHT: VIEW OF THE WORLD TRADE CENTER UNDER CONSTRUC-
TION, FROM ST. PAUL'S CHAPEL GRAVEYARD, 1970

OPPOSITE, LEFT: TOWER OF ST. PAUL'S CHAPEL RISES BETWEEN
THE TOWERS OF THE WORLD TRADE CENTER, 1977

OPPOSITE, RIGHT: TOWER OF ST. PAUL'S CHAPEL RISES ALONE

AFTER THE DESTRUCTION OF THE WORLD TRADE CENTER, 2001

CHINATOWN AND LOWER MANHATTAN FROM THE
MANHATTAN SIDE OF THE MANHATTAN BRIDGE, 1979
(RIGHT), SEPTEMBER 11, 2001 (OPPOSITE, LEFT), AND LATE
SEPTEMBER 2001 (OPPOSITE, RIGHT)

LEFT: VIEW SOUTH ALONG CENTER STREET TOWARD THE NEW
YORK COUNTY SURROGATE'S COURT, LOWER MANHATTAN,
SEPTEMBER 11, 2001

OPPOSITE: LOWER MANHATTAN SKYLINE FROM EXCHANGE
PLACE, SEPTEMBER 12, 2001

80 ABOVE: WRECKAGE OF THE WORLD TRADE CENTER, EAST RIVER, OCTOBER 2001. OPPOSITE: MEMORIALS, UNION SQUARE, SEPTEMBER 2001

VIEW SOUTH ALONG THE HUDSON RIVER FROM THE GEORGE WASHINGTON BRIDGE, WITH TWIN TOWERS IN THE DISTANCE, 1989